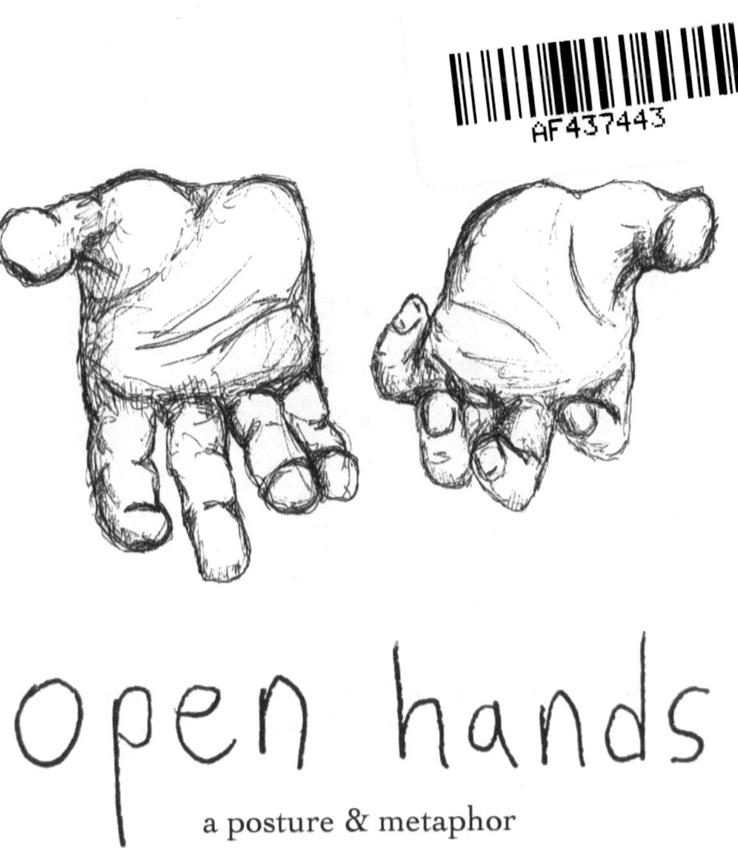

open hands

a posture & metaphor

second edition

by

ethan renoe

Dedicated to my cousin Tyler

a mind bursting with life and thoughts and humor and
rhythm and sly chuckles over tobacco-stained teeth.
There was a lot more that he owed to the world.
He owed us more of himself.
More of his thoughts and words.

More midnight pancakes at Denny's.

A poet and artist and letter writer,
he taught me how to be honest and cool.
He taught me how to dance.

Love you, cuz.

"Everything I've ever let go of
has claw marks on it."

-David Foster Wallace

My dad told me many times that,

"life is 10% what happens to you and 90% how you respond."

This book is about that 90%.

People often ask me why I have the word 'open'
tattooed in my palm.

I wrote this book so I don't have to answer that anymore.

The idea began 8 years ago.

I'm in college and have become best friends with Laura.
We do everything together:

homework in coffee shops,
watch movie matinees,
go to concerts,
attend trivia nights,
swing dance,
hit up holiday house parties

Laura is creative, hard working, and has curly golden wild
hair above energetic blue eyes.

And Laura is about to break my heart.

For two years, we were content being friends. But then,
after two years of close friendship, and seeing what an
amazing person Laura is, I decide she's not a friend —
she's the greatest person I've ever met.

I tell her I want to be more than friends and date,
or whatever.

She says no.

Everything inside of me hurts for days.
My arms hurt and my guts and my back
and the invisible parts of me all ache.

So I decide to talk to one of our professors about everything in me that's hurting because of Laura. He's the professor everyone talks to when they need dating advice.

We're sitting in the cafeteria and he begins: "Now, Ethan, you need to hold everything in an open hand."

He takes a pencil from his shirt pocket to illustrate this.

"Years ago, I met Sweet Sue and she was the most beautiful girl I'd ever seen," he says. "I wanted to grab onto her and hold her forever!"

"We dated and finally I married her. I thought I had closed my hand on her! I thought she was mine and she would never leave!

"But Ethan, five years ago, Sweet Sue got cancer. I thought God was going to take her out of my hand. And I didn't want to let go. I was holding onto her for dear life. I was scared God was going to wrestle her out of my fist.

"A year later she was in remission and got better. I got to keep her in my hand a little bit longer. But I learned a valuable lesson that day: There is nothing in this life that we can hold onto. There is nothing we ever get to fully 'close our fist on' in this life.

"So hold Laura in an open hand. If God wants to give her to you for a period of time (50 years or so) then He will keep her there. But trying to squeeze her, trying to close your fist on something God hasn't given you, is going to hurt you more than anyone else. And Laura will still be gone.

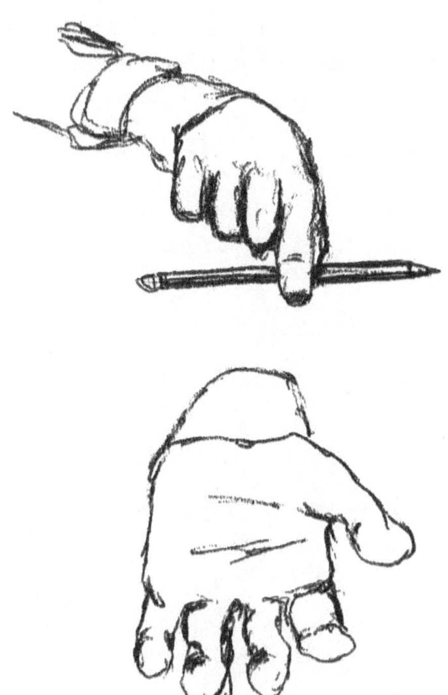

"God will do as He pleases either way; the only difference in the end is how you'll feel about it. So holding a posture of an open hand will make life much easier for *you*."

Then it got crazier.

"Ethan," he continued. "We have to hold *everything* in an open hand."

"Yah, I got it," I thought.

"About eight years ago, my daughter took her own life."

I felt my soul sink down from wherever souls normally rest down into my pelvis.

"I lost my only daughter. Sweet Sue and I mourned for years. But we learned to trust God, that God knew what God was doing by taking our daughter from us. Holding onto her in an angry, spiteful way would be fruitless. What would we accomplish? The Lord gives and the Lord takes away. It's a cute phrase until your own daughter is dead. Then it gets tested."

Suddenly I didn't like God.

I didn't like a God who would arbitrarily take things away like daughters and wives and Laura. My petty heartache was nothing compared to what I had just learned about this professor losing his child. But suddenly life seemed much larger and darker and like I was capable of falling much deeper into the abyss than I previously thought.

Laura never came back 'into my hand' and I had to move on, but the lesson from the professor was invaluable.

It's not only romantic escapades that we must hold with an open palm, but *everything*.

We are not guaranteed that anything will last forever.

Or even for our life.

Or even for a year.

Your home could explode.
Your best friend could move to Lisbon.
Your car could be set on fire (this happened to my
brother).
Your boyfriend could call things off the day after you two
shop for engagement rings.
Your child could get sick…or worse.

All this will happen whether you want it to or not;
the only difference will be your posture and response.

This is a book about that posture.
It's a book about response.
It's about good things coming and good things leaving.
And bad things coming and bad things leaving.

It's about treating other people with openness rather than
force, and accepting them as they come to you, not as you
wish they were.

Because this is the posture of God.

Recently, I heard a story from Andy Gullahorn about something he learned from God. This story has stuck with me for months, running through my mind at least once a day since I heard it.

Years ago, Andy was attending a certain church. This church began to fracture and ultimately split into two sides.

In the midst of the split, an older lady from the church dropped by for a visit with Andy. Toward the end of their coffee together, the older lady casually brought up the church.

"So which side will you stay with?"

He told her he was planning to go with such-and-such side.

The lady took this in.
Paused.
Pondered.
Then said,

"That...is the voice...of THE DEVIL!"

"...and that's how I knew I had made the right decision,"
Andy concluded with a laugh when he told this story.

Fast-forward a number of years. Andy continued to tell us
about various struggles he has with his faith. He said that
sometimes he's not sure he'll make it as a Christian.
Sometimes he wonders if he'll just drift away from Jesus.

But suddenly, continued Andy, one day in the midst of some
of his doubting, he felt like God brought to mind that
previous story about the old lady, yelling at him, telling him
that he was listening to the voice of the devil. I thought he
was just going to say that God was telling him, "NO! Don't
drift away from me! That would be the voice of the devil
leading you astray!"

But, he went on, he realized God brought that story to mind
to tell him something different. God was telling Andy that,
if he decided to walk away from God, God's posture toward
him would actually be the opposite of the old lady's.

God was saying, "Hey, if you decided to walk away from
me and leave your faith, I'd still walk with you. I'd see
where it takes you. Maybe it would be good for you.'"

This story just knocked the breath out of me.

What kind of God tells us, "You can walk away from me and still, I'll walk with you"?

What kind of God says, "You can ask anything. You can question everything. Let's just go through it together and see what happens"?

A God who really, *really* cares.

A God who is big enough to handle questions and searching.

A God who is curious, discovering things alongside us.

An open-handed *God*.

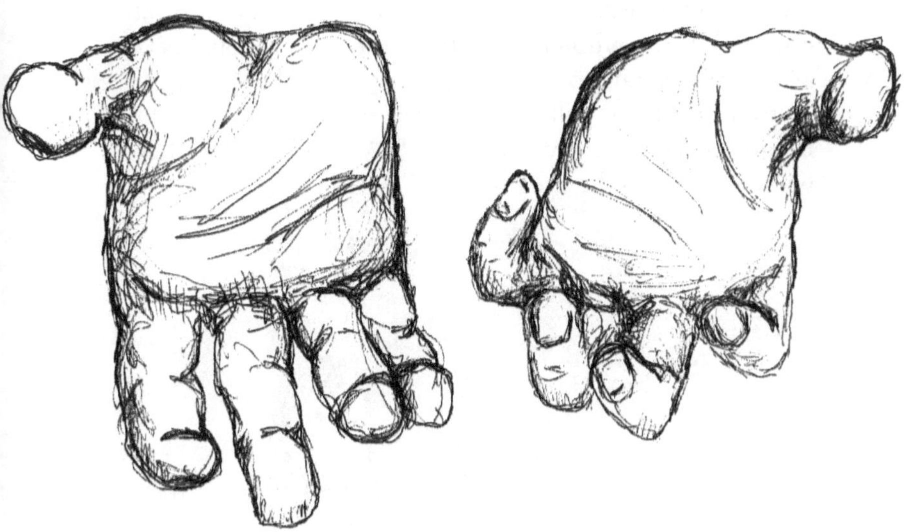

Because you will never get the best version of a human being by forcing them to bend the way you want.

Girlfriends who tell their boyfriends how to dress and act and what to like and how to spend their time do not create flourishing partners.

Lately a big one has been trying to force everyone who disagrees with us politically to see from *our* perspective. But think about it — have your political views shifted at all in the past 5 years? Is it possible they may be different 5 years from now? Or must we continue to force everyone to align with our exact ideology *right now*?

Parents who force their kids into the image they want often create children who grow up to be the most rebellious adults. How many of my students are forced to go to church, and later, will grow up to resent the church, simply because they were *forced* to attend? What if instead, they were *invited* into the great story of the universe?

Imagine a dating couple who simply enjoys each other as
they are, in the most open-handed form of romance
possible.

Imagine friends who don't guilt you for having your own
life, but allow themselves to fit gracefully into your time,
whenever your schedules align.

Imagine children who grow up with the freedom to explore
and be curious and fall down and get mud on their
forearms.

Can we also allow other people to hold their beliefs while
we hold ours? Can we hold *our* beliefs in an open hand,
knowing they may shift in the coming years?

Can we also hold the beliefs of
liberals,
conservatives,
libertarians,
anarchists,
transcendentalist poets,
communists,
fundamentalists,
and hippies
in an open hand, letting them exist in the world with the
same freedom, curiosity, and respect that you would like?

We can choose to let these beliefs air and breathe, or we can
try to force everyone on earth to see through the exact same
lens that we do.

We can try to bend them into the image of ourself.

Even Jesus doesn't do this in the gospels. He answers most questions with questions, not definitive sound bites.

He never simplistically declares, "Yah, I'm gonna have to side with the Herodians on this current issue."

He sings hymns
and tells stories
and recites poems
and plays with mud and sand
and pulls from the Hebrew Bible
and heals people
and gives dignity to the sinners,
but mostly, Jesus eats with folks.

Jesus is the open-handed God of the open table.

Brennan Manning describes God as loving us "unconditionally…as you are, and not as you should be, because none of us are as we should be."

But do we love one another this way?

Do we love our children as they are,
not as we want them to be?

Do we love our spouses as they look
and not as we wish they would look?

Do we love our friends on their own schedule,
not the one we wish they had?

Do we love those we disagree with?

It is, in the tireless and trite maxim,
much easier said than done.

Do you hold people in an open hand,
the way you want them to hold you?

Open hands cannot force or manipulate
situations or people.

Relationships are like rivers. Some run their course in your life quickly and are gone. Others are like the Amazon and will run firm and long alongside your own river for your entire life.

Other rivers may change shape and course as they run.

A friend gets married and has a baby. Their river is still in your life, but the flow has changed. The landscape morphs. The flora and fauna which attend to the waters may differ but still your rivers run.

At times people have left my life against my will. They may simply stop returning messages or invites to get together, despite my multiple efforts. They may move away and you drift apart.

But just as you can't force a river to run, you can't force people into your life.

Some of us may ponder this and want other people to hold us tighter. Maybe there is an anxiety about being let go, because we as children felt unwanted. Maybe you read these words and want to hold tightly to everyone in your life, and want all of them to hold you just as tightly. You probably think—with the absolute purest intentions—that this is loving. You want to love your people and you want them to love you.

But holding and being held in an open hand requires trust. It requires you to relinquish control over others.

Are you tired of trying to get them to close their fist on you?

Over a decade ago, I was head over heels for a different girl. She fascinated me like a muse. I wrote her songs and poetry and invited her on hikes and adventures.

But she didn't feel the same way.

And I wasted many hours trying to convince her why she should like me.

I tried to argue her into wanting a romance with this nitwit.

But that's not how romance and desire and attraction and love work…is it?

You don't argue people into holding you in their fist; You hold yours open and see if they stay. You seek people who are also open to the world and see if they want to let you rest a while in *their* palm.

It's scary because it necessarily means you're not in control.

It means you're letting the other decide the future of your relationship. Will this river end here, or will it run on and gain strength? It's out of your hands…so to speak.

You can invite a woman on a date but you can't make her say yes. You can chat with a handsome stranger at a party but you can't force him to be attracted to you. All you can do is present yourself, openly and honestly, and see who decides to stay.

And the little secret is, the right ones will always stay.
The right things will always stick.

Earlier this year I bought my first home.

It was an exhausting process, as I put in 11 offers on places, only to meet rejection after rejection. With each place though, there were small exceptions I would have had to make.

This one doesn't have great light.
This one is ten minutes further from work than I'd prefer.
This one is just a weird shape, but we'll still go for it.

But then I found another.

I looked at it somewhat hopelessly—it was too good to be true. Surely everyone else would be bidding on this one.

The windows look out at a park.
The whole interior was recently redone.
Black granite countertops.
Ten minutes from my work.
Ideal layout, with plenty of storage
Plenty of parking for guests.
Natural light.
Well within my price range.
Walking trails.
Easy access to a highway to zip up to downtown.
Shops 3 minutes away.
Super low HOA.

It was a nice dream, but it would never materialize.

But three days later my realtor called and told me we were under contract.

Thirty days later I was signing the papers on my dream place.

"How many offers did you put in?" asked the woman at the title office.

"12," I told her.

"But was this the best one out of all 12?"

I thought about it and realized that yes, out of the dozen offers I'd put in, this was by far the best for me in every conceivable way.

"That's how it always seems to work out," she told me with a smile.

I wondered if that's how most of life is supposed to happen. You can force the wrong thing, or let the right one come when the time is right. You can grab with your hands at things that just aren't landing right, or you can trust that the best is still on its way.

There are many seasons of life I look back on with a sepia-tinted fondness. I felt more alive. The sky was bluer. Poetry hit in deeper places. Adventure called with a bullhorn.

One summer, I lived on a beach with no home but the sand and waves — and it was the best summer of my life.

I was devastated when it ended and didn't want to return to *school*, land of buttoned-up, tucked-in shirts. I didn't want to focus on papers rather than paddling out to crab rock and poking jellyfish and diving off docks and balancing our way down forgotten train tracks.

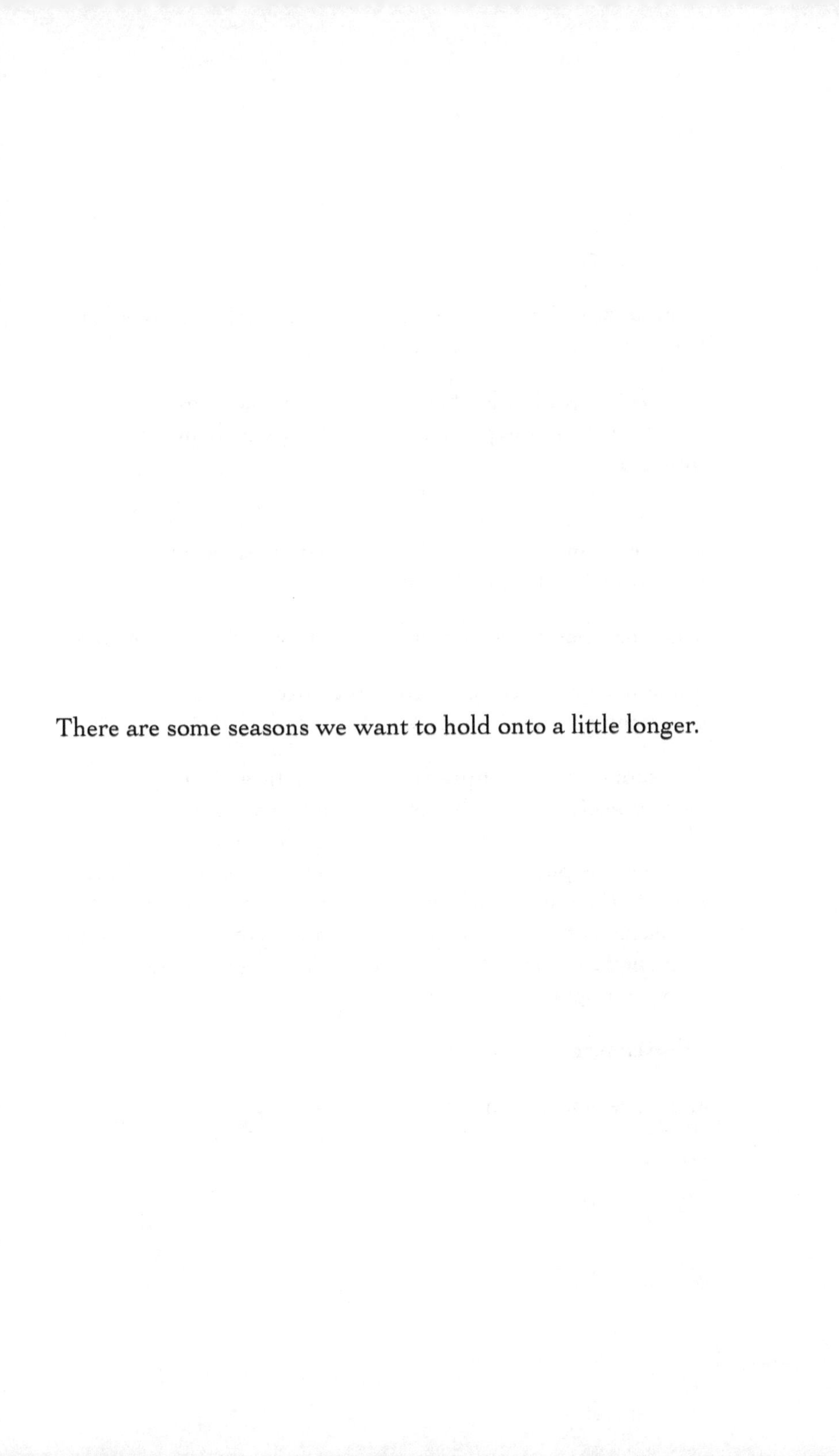

There are some seasons we want to hold onto a little longer.

Even today, if someone gave me a time machine, I wouldn't hesitate to rush back to that summer.

But, as far as I know, there are no time machines. You're stuck in the present and moving slowly into the future.

So you can try to hold onto the past like retired porch warriors reminiscing on 'the good old days,' or you can keep your hands open for the inevitable future.

Time marches cruelly on, no matter how tightly you grip it.

Sometimes we need to let go of the past so we can receive the future.

The sooner we are at peace with the nature of time, the more gracefully we will move through the various seasons of our lives. Many single people long to be married. Married people are dying to have kids. and so on. But the Apostle Paul, in 1 Corinthians 7, urges us to be content in all seasons of life, wherever we are at. If you're single, enjoy singleness. If you're married but childless, enjoy the time with your spouse.

All seasons come and go,

and all seasons, as they arrive and depart,

are a gift.

You can rush the gift or let the giver give.

This was the lesson learned by one of our oldest fathers, Abraham.

God came to him and told him that he and his wife Sarai
would have a son. The only catch is, they're already
geriatric and well past the child-bearing age.

Sarai laughs at God.

But God even made a covenant with Abraham, cut a bunch
of animals in half, shed a ton of blood, just to show how
serious he was about keeping this promise to Abraham.

All Abraham had to do was wait.

Wait and receive.

But ten years after the promise was made to him, they were getting impatient. So rather than trust the promise that was made to them ten years prior, they decide to take a slave girl named Hagar and make her have Abraham's child.

They were trying to force the gift from God's hand, rather than to wait and receive.

So Abraham impregnates Hagar (likely against her will), and as a result, Hagar begins to despise them. She flees from Abraham and Sarai, and this is where it gets interesting. Rather than follow the narrative of the powerful patriarch, the story follows Hagar out into the wilderness. God meets her and tells her that she is seen.

She then names God "The One Who Sees Me."

God is the One who *sees* the abused slave who has escaped into the wilderness.

God is the One who made a promise to Abraham, the powerful and rich caravan owner, and all Abraham had to do was be patient.

But instead, Abraham forced God's hand, created a son by his own means, and disrupted his entire family. He not only ruined the life of the slave woman, but of his own son he had with her as well.

He rushed what he wanted by force, devastating the lives of others and himself in the process.

Sometimes, when God doesn't move fast enough for us,
we start doing God's job for Him.

Later, when he's 100 years old, God finally gives him and Sarai a child.

Maybe one of the lessons God is teaching in this narrative is: "I have a plan and you don't know what it is. You can wait and see how it unfolds in beauty like a flower unfurling itself in the springtime, or you can rush it, force it, use your puny human means to force the flower open yourself. You can prematurely peel back the petals of the rose and kill the entire plant in the process. You can destroy the lives of others in the process."

Instead, wait. Receive.

Open hands can't take, they can only receive.
Open hands can't hold onto things longer than they should.

Does the flower force the sun to shine down on it, or does it simply wait to receive the light?

Can it make the clouds send water to nourish its roots, or does it just trust God to send the rain?

Maybe this is part of what Jesus meant when He told us not to worry—God sees the flowers of the field and dresses them better than a king in all his splendor.

And the flowers don't do a dang thing to work for it.

Or maybe it's like the writer of Psalm 103, who said that mortals are like flowers of the field. We don't get what we need because we force it, but because ultimately, everything we will *ever* get comes as a gift. Did you construct your own body inside your mother? Did you select the time period in which you'd be born, and all the technology and opportunities that would be available to you?

Yes, you've worked for a lot You've accomplished a lot. I've gotten degrees, not because I sat around and let them come to me, but because I worked for them and paid a handsome chunk of money to educational institutions.

But did I make my own brain, or did I decide that I wouldn't be born with mental handicaps or impairments?

Everything is a gift and you can't force or rush gifts.

Being a hopeless romantic, I have often written songs or poems for ladies who caught my fancy. They inspire songs and lines and prose, or something invisibly connecting me to them prompts me to buy them flowers on the way to a date, or to pick up a little candy they like.

But there have been one or two I can think of
who did it wrong.

"Write me a song," said one girl,
        and suddenly I didn't want to.

"Buy me flowers…I love it when a guy buys me flowers."

The demand, or the force, robs the gift of its beauty.

Part of the beauty of receiving a gift is the very nature of it:

the surprise,
the *receiving*,
the lack of all force,
and the freedom to let the giver simply give, out of their
own joy, not out of obligation, or simply to fulfill a request.

Something you pull out of someone is not a gift.

Forcing your slave to have your son is not a gift.

Telling your boyfriend to write you a song is not a gift.
(and it would hardly be considered an honest song if he did)

Maybe we are bad at receiving gifts.

Maybe we are impatient.

Maybe we are scared of not being in control of
the things that come our way.

Maybe we are clenching our fists in anger.

Maybe we are addicted to self-sufficiency.

Maybe someone needs to tell us to sit down
and hold our hands open.

I read in Bob Goff's book *Love Does* that as a lawyer, when he meets with convicts, he makes them sit and answer questions with their palms open and face up. He says that people are more honest when they have their hands open, their palms exposed.

In some ways, it's a vulnerable position. The human tendency is to put the hands down, to hide or cover them. We cross our arms or put our hands in our pockets or make fists.

But when you're sitting before someone with your hands open, you feel more exposed.

It's true — try it.

Try to tell someone a lie while holding your hands open before them.

It'll feel weird (weirder than lying already feels).

It's an unnatural position to hold.

I read *Love Does* years ago, when it first came out, and I decided to try implementing that practice in my personal prayer time. So I began sitting in a chair, reading my Bible for a minute, then sitting with my eyes closed, feet uncrossed, and palms open and up.

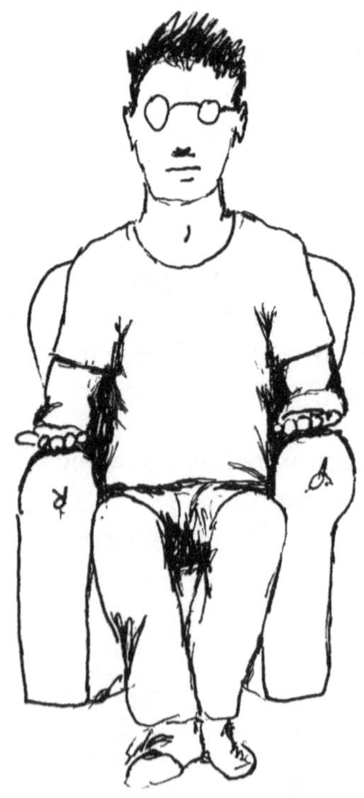

And EVERYTHING changed!

Just kidding.

Nothing insanely magical happened.

But the small physical act of holding my hands open before God, rather than palm-down on the armrests put my mind in a slightly different posture. It made me feel slightly more vulnerable than if I had a *grip* on the armrests, holding on like I have any control.

A seminary professor once said,

"The body responds well to metaphor."

Ask a group of people to pray and instinctively, they all lean
forward, fold their hands any number of ways, and close
their eyes.

But try getting real weird with it sometime.

Try getting on the floor and lying flat on your face
like a log.

Try folding down atop your knees with your forehead to the
floor; you could even hold your palms up on the floor.

Try pacing while praying.

Jews at the Wailing Wall rock back and forth while praying.

The origins are uncertain, but some Jews point to Psalm 35, which says,

> All my bones shall say,
> "Who is like You, Lord?"

Another legend describes a historical moment when printed Torahs were less common, so one by one, men would come up to a scroll on a table, bend over to read a passage, and go to the back of the line. Thus, it created the association of reading and ruminating on scripture with the act of bending and rising, which Jews today do while praying or studying or meditating on Torah.

Observing this, Muslims were instructed by Mohammed
not to move, or even fidget while praying (Though later this
was reversed, as long as you don't imitate any 'non-Muslim
movements'…whatever those are).

Point is, every culture gives a lot of meaning to bodily movement.

Our Western, American tradition seems to be more focused on the mind. Come to most churches today, and the bulk of the service revolves around the sermon. Sure, there are songs and some weirdos may raise their hands during these, and there's the occasional communion snack'n'sip, but the whole body is certainly not involved in worship.

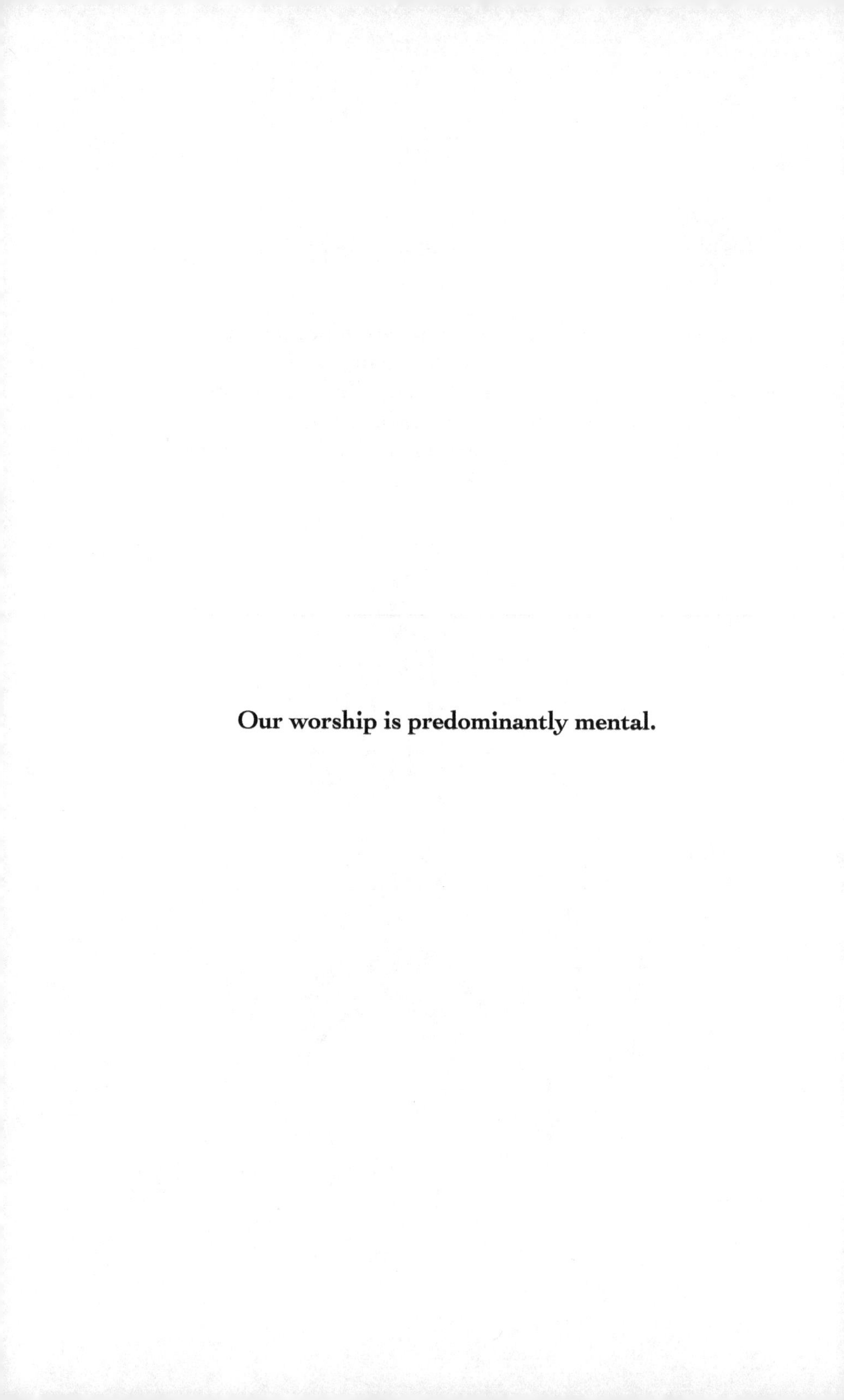

Our worship is predominantly mental.

Until you begin to look at the Bible and find that worshipers are repeatedly instructed to use their *bodies* to cry out to God.

Psalm 95 invites us to "worship and bow down; let us kneel before the Lord, our Maker!"

Psalms 28, 63, 68, 88, 119, 134, 141, and 143 all mention raising our hands to the Lord, as do verses in Lamentations, 1 Timothy, Luke, Ezra, and Habakkuk.

As western, intellectual elites, I wonder if we read these
texts and think, *Ok, I'm mentally raising my hands to the Lord,*
instead of,
you know…
doing it.

Try it.

Maybe you're too shy to go to church and actually bow
down, or even raise your hands. Try it in your bedroom.
Make sure you close the curtains so no one peeks in and
thinks you're one of those weird *religious* people though.

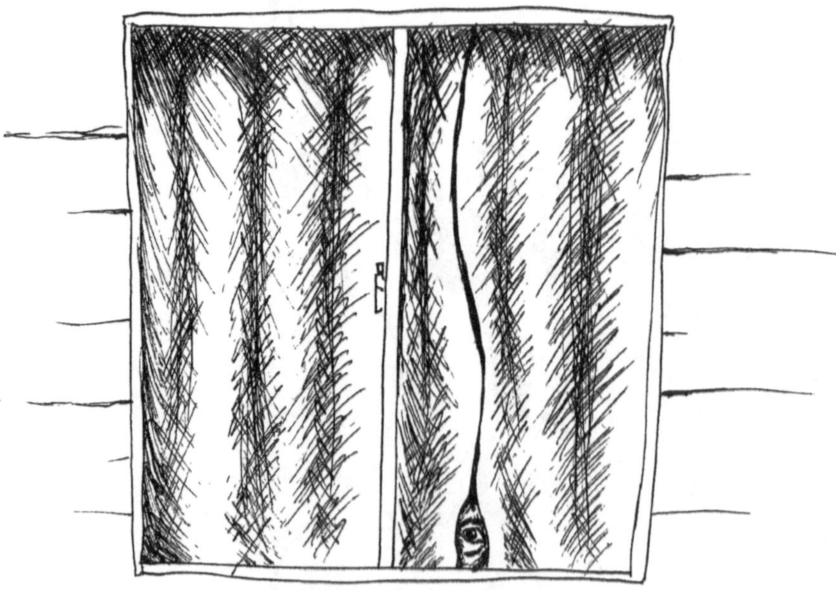

Prayer and worship are not just about the words we use.

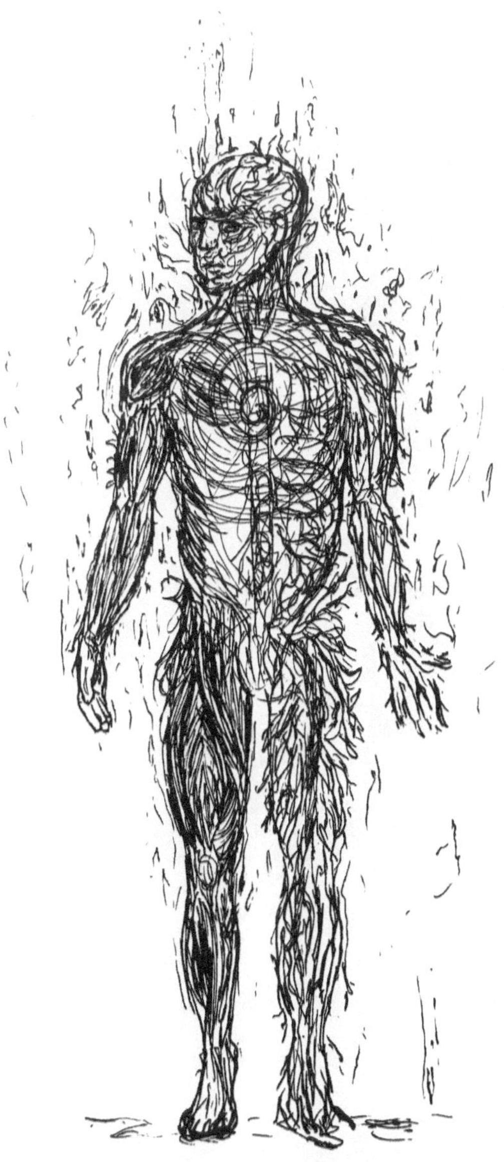

They are about the whole body.

The body responds well to metaphor.

The body is a metaphor.

When you are bent down with your head on the carpet, you
are symbolically offering your neck to whoever you bow to.
Historically, you'd offer this gesture to a king, saying that
'my life is in your hands. Do with it what you will.'

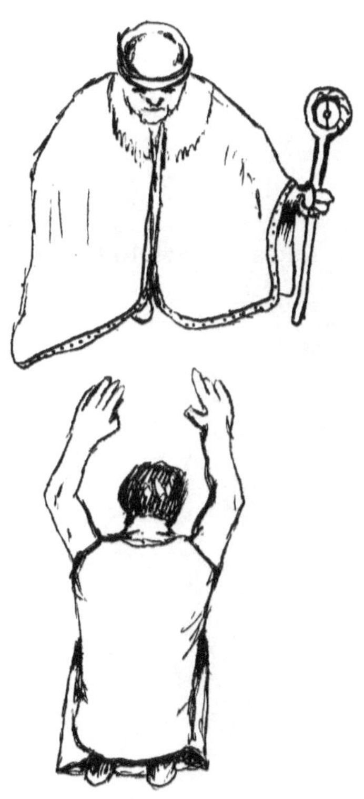

And that takes us back to the beginning.

Because no matter what, life will do what it will to us.

God is up to something big with our lives

and deaths

and work
and hobbies
and favorite movies
and books
and recreation league sports
and church gatherings
and friendships
and people we don't like
and holey socks
and romances
and pets
and their deaths
and sleep
and car breakdowns
and Homeowners Associations
and even our sins
and addictions
and injuries
and seasons
and emotions
and families
and conversations
and laughter
and possessions
and good meals
and bad coffee
and microwaves
and sunsets
and pants
and paperwork,

and we don't always know what it is, but it all matters.

And we are only given the option of how we respond
to this big thing God is up to.

And when I realized this was true, I took my tattoo machine, popped a needle in, and wrote the word 'open' in my palm, as a reminder.

And as a symbol.
Because the body is a metaphor, remember?

So now, people often ask me why I have the word 'open' tattooed in my palm, and now this book is their answer.

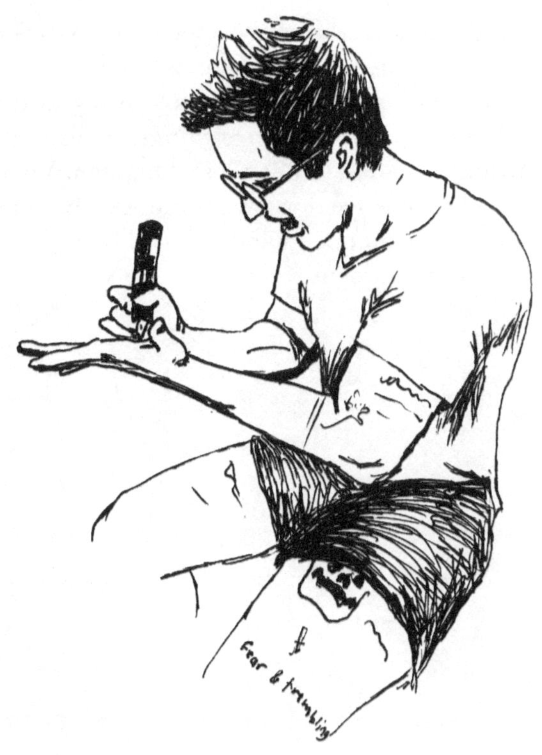

We are placed into a world where a lot of things are not how we would like them, and we are only given the option to receive them with grace or bitterness; with gratitude or complaint. We can work to change things, to make them better, but things we don't like will still happen. We will lose things and people we don't want to lose. But maybe, by holding all things in an open hand, we will be more ready for life, however it happens to us.

And just maybe,
we will catch some unexpected goodness
with those same open hands.

e

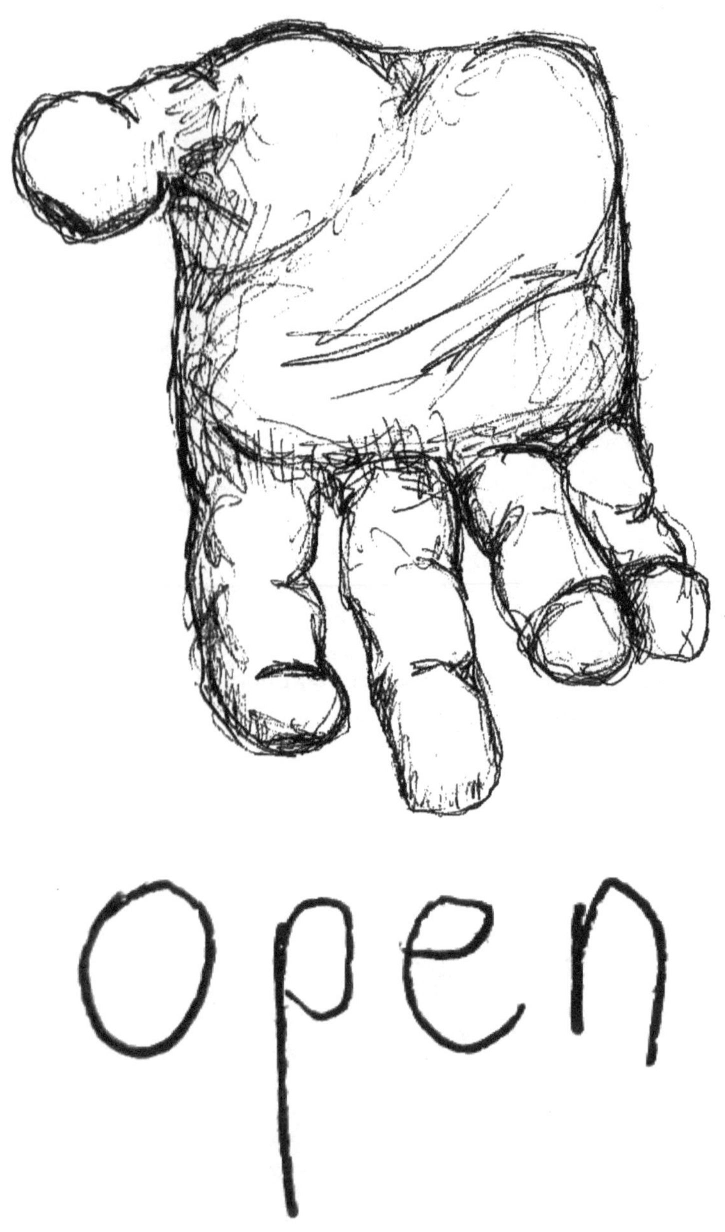

open

You are dust and breath.

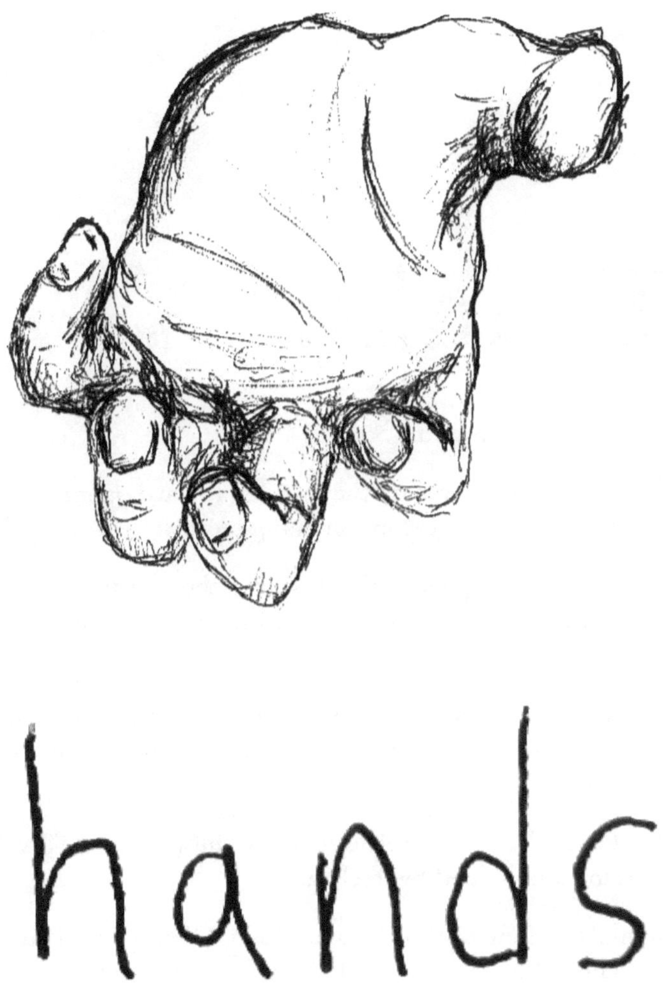

hands

Let go of your life.

Thanks.

Thanks for reading this book.

Thanks for joining me on the journey toward openness, toward a posture of reception and generosity.

Thanks to all the people who inspired the words of this book; I know who you all are and I'm grateful you *gave* much of yourself to me, to us.

Thanks to the artists Boundaries, Silent Planet, and Chris Renzema—the background soundtrack to the writing of this book.

Thanks to Michael and Andy and all the guys at RTS who loved me and helped me feel again.

Thanks to Mandee(y?), Krista, Noah, Dieo, Angela, and Michelle, who read this book in advance and gave me the most helpful feedback and correction.

Other books by Ethan

How to Understand the Entire Universe, Part 1
self-explanatory

Bad Timing
bittersweet love stories and what I learned from them

If you could haunt your house forever
a collection of odd & eerie stories

The New Lonely
finding intimacy in the age of isolation

Time Kills All Things
a collection of 300 essays

Now let me find a stopping place
a decade of poetry, 2008-2018

Leaving Weather
Expressions, images, and wanderings

More at ethanrenoe.com

yo.